I0427927

The Little Book
To
Push Through
Pain

Denisia J. Hockley

Copyright © 2012

All rights reserved.

www.littlebookseries.us
ISBN-13:9781514849637
ISBN-10:1514849631

CONTENTS

Denisia Hockley

The Little Book
To
Push Through Pain

We all experience pain of all types and in all sorts of places: Some tolerate/deal with it better than others: Some put it on display while others hide it well. Do not be fooled by the outward expression of pain or apparent 'lack of' – You rarely really know other peoples' stuff!

When we say your pain is mostly in your head we are not saying it is not real! We are not saying it is not physically debilitating or that you are making it up or exaggerating. The science of pain is fascinating and empowering!

Once you grasp the concept of **No Brain**

No Pain you open up a whole new world of power and control over your own body and mind.

Come with me on a journey of discovery; open your mind; let go of past beliefs and limitations! (Reading Magical Mind will enhance this experience)

What do you really have to lose?

This book is in no way meant to minimize or trivialize your pain (for the record: I am no stranger to these issues both professionally and personally. Everything I tell you to do, I practice myself! It works but you have to make the effort and do the exercises.). Two years ago I had surgery that should have been simple but poor choice of surgeon, a botched job = constant pain.

More recently; three months ago I fell while on roller blades and shattered both wrists! Yup both of them! At first I was in the ER laughing and making jokes because I had no idea how extensive the damage was: I was in pain but my brain was not taking it really seriously, a combination of shock, denial and just not knowing.

My brain had not got the full message!!.

It was not until later that night, with both hands and arms in casts that I started to realize how incapacitated I was: could not scratch my nose, feed myself and a whole lot of personal things I do not have to spell out! Of course in this space of time the physiology of the damage had not changed very much but the realizations in my head were bouncing all over the place and of course with this came extreme increases in pain levels.

Now of course I 'am' the queen of pain therapy, literally wrote the book (this paragraph kinda wrote itself while I was going through all this, so of course I had to add it to the book). However! I am, as I have always said, just a mere humanoid like you. So before working my magic I still had to go through processes, maybe I did spend a little less time in the transitioning, but still had to go through them.

The first few days the pain was off the charts, in fact asking us to rate it from 1 to 10 is inappropriate, the medics did not like me saying "It's 597…and I will tell you when it gets down to a 10!" From now on all my clients, at least, will get to rate from 1 to 100!

Of course there was more than one type of pain going on at that time, there was the constant, the background physical pain that never went away (It is still there to some extent but I have shut off the 'brain-pain' message).

There is the other more important pain though, the one I respect! The one I am not going to shut down because for one thing, 'I know me!', if I do not have any pain reminders I will do the things that I am not allowed to do 'yet'…not just because I'm stubborn but largely because I forget. I am a very active, independent person which means I literally and metaphorically do all my own lifting.

I am not supposed to be lifting, pulling or pushing more than 400 grams/2 pounds with one hand! Seriously! I'm sure everything weighs way more than that. For a while there, any door that said "PULL" was effectively saying, "Denisia you are not welcome here!!!!"

So when I go to lift, pull or push something over the weight that my injuries are ready for, thankfully, I get sharp O.T.T. pain that tells me to stop and respect my current limitations if I do not want them to go on forever. I'm learning how far I can push things so as to speed my recovery but not inhibit it.

Mostly though, people get used to the 'injured' profile and do a lot less than they really could… I am not minimizing the fact that it hurts, I know (even now while I'm typing I'm using joints and muscles that would rather be left alone but I have it on good authority that typing and using a mouse is ultimately good physical therapy so I do not need the pain message and I do need to get on with my life.

When you rest too much or move your joints/bones/whatever less than you should/could you cause atrophy (loss of strength/abilities/muscle etc.) and make the cost of your original injury go up.

The surgeon told me I will probably get some 'artharitus'.. We will see about that! *I can't even spell the word*!

As for osteoporosis! not interested in that one either. Now of course I (as I have said before) am a mere humanoid and those things are highly likely to try and invade my life BUT I certainly will not go without a fight! This is a good spot to mention supplements, exercise, and balanced healthy eating, nothing fanatical just consistent good habits most of the time. Don't waste good money on a truck load of supplements without doing your homework. And try not to leave these good habits until after you break a few bones, fortunately I have lead a reasonably healthy (without being miserable) lifestyle in terms of nutrition and exercise for a few years now so I only have to tweak a few things.

Simply put, use the 'no brain no pain' techniques I have given you appropriately but respect that sudden sharp pain that tell you (me) stop! But you have to work out where the line is between pushing the boundaries and re-injuring yourself! Other than athletes very few people are going to push themselves too far!

The early stages (couple days couple years- your choice) are where we (me) just cry, complain and feel miserable – again....humans! It's OK! We have to adjust... you don't tell someone who's cat just got squished by a car that they will get over it and replace it in the near future!!! You allow time for a normal healthy emotional response. So we have our cry, get angry and chew over the mind wracking question WHY?!! Then we get up, get back in the ring, and focus on what we can do rather than what we cannot. And no, that doesn't mean you won't revisit the negative, depressive aspects of your situation but if you read my books and use my tools to understand yourself and your brain, you will recognize what you are doing, have your little mope or tantrum or both (because it's good to get them damn emotions out so they do not fester) and get back on the horse.

Can't help wondering if some sort of universal plan is making sure I write with authenticity.

Anyway it is what it is

I have a number of clients right now who deal with pain on a regular basis; they are pretty much getting on track to push through it to a more comfortable more active life.

There are people born without the wiring that tells their brain to feel pain: you want that disorder you say? Seriously?

Have you ever had a paper cut on your finger and it did not even hurt until you knew it was there.
Imagine if you're an athlete and you break an ankle but your brain doesn't receive the message (pain response) so you keep on running….you end up with much worse damage than a sprained ankle.

So how about someone who has damaged nerves in their leg; everything medically that can be done has been. They have their walking stick, they know what they can and can't do… Brain got the memo! Message received! We have damage and we have done everything we can to fix it! So why does he need to continue feeling pain; well maybe if he forgets about the damage he might toss the walking stick and start playing football. What if I say you can learn not to feel the pain (or at the very least to reduce those pain messages considerably). More on this later…

Twelve years ago I had an operation on my foot (in hindsight I probably shouldn't have had the surgery; whatever!) anyway the surgeon told me no more dancing, skiing, toss the high heels and wear crappy old granny shoes; on top of that he gave me a walking stick and told me that this was now my life!

Worst of all, I bought it! I believed the 'professional' and for three months I was a bad tempered girl with granny shoes, a walking stick and no life.

Then one day I got angry; REALLY damn angry (might have been better had I not been at work that day).

I threw the stick across the room, let out a lot of expletives and said NO! F*** the experts! I put on my heels, I went dancing and skiing and everything else I have always done, and yes it did hurt.

It hurt like hell but I was stubborn, pig-headed and damn angry that I had bought into the whole 'Disabled profile'. I don't remember how long it took before the pain went... I kinda forgot about it because I was too busy getting my normal life back. I am not saying that this can work in all situations but I am saying that this did happen! You will losing nothing by trying!

Sometimes some well executed, focused 'anger energy' can overcome some obstacles.

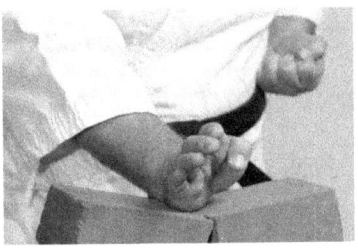

I have also had to develop some sort of general mental pain methods because I can't take pain meds (won't bore you with that story). Necessity is a great teacher. One thing we do know is that being idle makes pain worse OR more accurately diversion tactics interfere with brain-pain communication.

Ever been sick and something comes up, one of the kids has an accident and you have to tend to them or some other crises happens and while you are in emergency mode you forget about your stuffed back or torn rotator cuff and you do what needs to be done.... Because you had to!

Bob Marley once said "you don't know how strong you can be until strong is your only choice"

You did not have time to focus on your own pain. I have a process I teach my clients (usually after I have taught them a lot of the stuff that you will find in 'Magical Mind'; because a lot of the things I am going to teach you now require a 'willing suspension of disbelief'.

Some of these concepts may challenge your belief system, but just try it, what do you have to lose!

More things in this universe are true Than just what you can see, feel, understand and believe!.

In fact, I recently heard that researchers in the USA are applying my methods but in a very simple way. They are using video games to 'cure' or at least distract from pain: surprise, surprise, it works.

You will understand why by the time you finish this book AND supplement it with The Little Book for your Magical Mind.

In the late 1800s some other crazy medical minds started to talk about invisible alien entities that invade our bodies causing us great sickness and often death.

These insane physicians tried to convince people that it was these invisible entities that were the primary cause of all ailments and even death. Crazier still was the way they suggested beating this alien invasion – soap and water.

It's a wonder they did not get burned at the stake for such insanity.

Of course today we treat 'germs' with more than soap and water but where would we be if those 'nut jobs' had not risked their credibility to expound such insane theories.

Your Body is Both a Magical & Measurable Entity
(No Brain No Pain)

Your mind is magical but this is not magic;

it is Brain Science and it works!

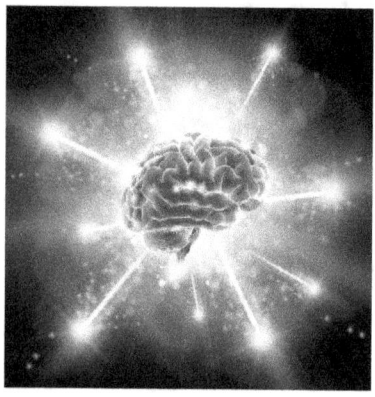

The process: Take this slow and work on each step until you **'get it!'**

Sit in a chair; I want to work first on getting you to know your body and heighten your physical awareness (and control)! So start with the butt muscle;

You already know how to flex and release your butt muscle. Do you know exactly how you control this muscle group? Or is it more like you **just think it and it happens**? Practice that a few times. Of course a medical professional can explain the dynamics of brain impulses, action potentials and a whole lot of science gobbledygook BUT to us mere mortals, it really does seem like we just think it and it happens.

Now go for something a little harder, lock in you abdominals (your core) this is really hard to start with but keep trying until you get it (bonus: while you do this you are working on your six pack: I have one now and its really kinda cool).

Practice locking, holding and releasing. Try to build up to a whole minute hold and you will start to get rock hard abbs (Like mine) If you're struggling. any gym junky will give you some tips on how to do it.

Now for a visual: Again sitting in the chair I want you to play with a muscle you can see: tense and release a top thigh muscle and watch it move:

Think it, move it; think it; move it; Even Homer can do that one.

OK now for a leap of faith, think of a muscle inside where you can't see…or feel…..Throats are good for this. Especially if you have ever had anxiety (see Little Book to Annihilate Anxiety) and you have felt that scary tightening of the throat brought about by a fear response.

Remember you will not get any proof that it is happening so do it quite a few times.

With enough practice you may become vaguely aware that it is working;   more than likely you will just have to believe me! BUT since it worked on the ones you can feel and see, doesn't common sense and logic tell you that it is working on ones you cannot see.

Just because you can't prove something does not mean it is not happening!

Can you prove there are no purple polar bears?

I won't give you the rest of the exercise just yet because I want you to get this down pat first. So keep practicing these exercises until you understand that your brain actually can control all your muscles etc.

Let's talk about pain medication:

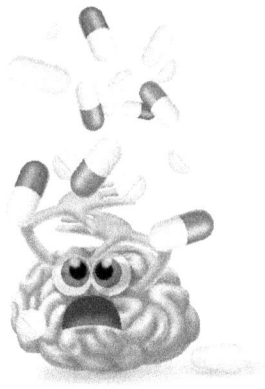

In the long term pain medication does not work! You think it does: especially if you have been on it for a long time, but truth is your taking more and stronger meds than you used to and you're still in pain!

Pain meds have ruined (but not permanently) your pain tolerance. A bit like overuse of antibiotics weakens your body's ability to fight off disease. Long term use of narcotics like morphine can have a paradoxical effect in that it actually increases your pain but you don't know this; you just think your pain is growing and you need more and more meds.

Sorry to disillusion you but this is true!

I have recorded a CD-Therapy for pain which I based on hypnotherapy that I used while working in a Pain Clinic in Los Angeles:

A fascinating fact: A lot of my clients were Mexican and I had to use an interpreter, I would have thought the communication barrier would have diminished the effects of my hypnotherapy! But it still worked!

These were long term chronic pain patients. The results were pretty good. You can get this and other CDs at   www.littlebookseries.us

(This little pain-man is the star of the pain CD Therapy script. You will see what this means when you listen to the CD)

Part two of the earlier exercise:

(DO NOT START ON THIS IF YOU HAVE NOT PRACTICED THE FIRST PART)

I want you to find a pain that you are experiencing **now**: focus on it with everything you have and **MAKE IT WORSE!**

Yup. I said increase your pain!   Trust me on this:

Your brain is actually highly experienced in increasing your pain levels in various situations. In fact we are pretty good at increasing lots of undesirable stuff in our lives; just by using our brain the wrong way (if you doubt me think about how often you make your issues worse just by worrying and stressing over them).

So practice this over and over and over again: increase - hold – and return to where it was.

We are talking long term pain and long term results so please resist the urge to go to the next stage too soon: I want you to practice this for as long as it takes for you to feel the exhilaration of knowing you can control your body in this way.

Even though it hurts; really do look on the up side of this!

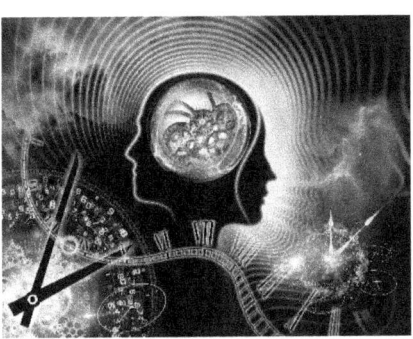

When you reach this point (not before) you are ready to have a little talk to your brain: You have established that your brain controls every part of your body! You have just provided yourself with definitive evidence that you can increase your pain levels:

Logical conclusion?   Think about it?

It's not rocket science!

You can now start to reduce; turn down, the levels, of your pain right?!

Remember mentally getting rid of the pain may not mean you can throw away your stick or get out of the wheelchair (it doesn't necessarily mean you can't either) but essentially we are saying that you know what you need to know about the damage; you do what is necessary, like not running on a sprained ankle:

So Brain…we got the memo! We know what the pain message was for and now we do not need it!

You now have the tools to minimize your pain but like everything else in your toolbox: It only works if you use it!

When pain pays off!

A touchy subject: It's here to help you not to offend you!

When you have a compensation case or any injury situation, illness or pain that makes you dependent on a pension or involves litigation: You will not fully recover until you get out from under the

'Obligation to suffer'.

NO I am not saying you are faking it; on the contrary it is because you are an honest person that your brain is going to provide you with as much pain and discomfort as possible so that you won't feel like a fraud.

Remember when you wanted a day off work so you called in sick: by the end of the day your throat was swollen and you felt like crap. Essentially you felt guilty for taking a sick day so your brain made it right by making you genuinely sick.

Before you go down any medico legal roads make sure you're up for the journey because it's a long rough trip: sometimes unavoidable, especially if someone has damaged you physically and you need to make them pay at least for the repair work. Do what you need to do but make sure the ends are worth the means and that you use these pain techniques to minimize your discomfort along the way.

Another important element of pain profiles that you need to consider: Is there a payoff to being sick or in pain' (physically, psychologically, whatever) does it allow you to avoid other issues, challenges or even just moving forward with life.

If you woke up tomorrow with no injuries, no illness, and no pain: what would you do with your time? How would you plan the rest of your life? Be honest is this daunting or scary? Maybe you and your disability have been supporting each other so long that life without it would be scary…..

Not saying that this applies to you….. But it might… just give it some thought!

Do you get help, sympathy, attention that you would not get if you were healthy?

When you were a kid did you take second (or no) place because you had a sick sibling? Did she get all the attention because of her disability and were you left to fend for yourself, or maybe you had to give up a lot of your time looking after her needs. (See Sick Sibling Syndrome [SSS] in Little Scientist).

Were there times when you actually had to be sick to get the attention you needed, and had a perfect right to, from your parents? Or maybe the only time they stopped fighting was when you were sick and they had to take care of you.

Just some thoughts to ponder! A lot in life that does not seem to have a reason or make any sense actually does have an explanation buried in the complex mechanics of your mind: A lot like getting a new computer; everything in it makes sense once you learn how it thinks and what the relevant connections are.

There are actually extreme psychological disorders where people physically injure themselves or their children to get some sort of perceived love and attention. We won't go into that here but you can Google it (Munchausen's disorder) if you're interested.

For this to happen these people have clearly suffered immense rejection, neglect and abandonment issues.

One of the many tragedies of abusive, neglectful or even ignorant parenting!.

I am not saying you have this disorder but it is VERY common for people to *unconsciously* get sick or injured because they are so starved for love and attention.

Self-awareness and personal insight are powerful tools.

Rejection is always more painful

when it mirrors that

Which we reject in ourselves!

There are many levels of pain; many ways to be broken: Some might say physical pain is the easiest one to deal with; at least you have something to show; something people understand.

It is similar to physical abuse; turn up at the police station with a black eye and your situation is immediately understood: go to the same place and explain the emotional abuse that stops you leaving the family home and the answer you get may be

"Just leave".

Many years ago I had a man come into my practice with his wife, whom he wanted "fixed, because she was 'mad'..." He was a big guy; in stature, his position (high as you can get in the legal system actually); he was also narcissistic, etc. etc. ….. Anyway, it turned out that he had brought his wife into the city with him and locked her in his car for the day while he worked!

That sounds bad right?   Think about it for a moment… think about your car….. The locking mechanism… are you with me yet?

So why didn't she just get out of the car? The psychological abuse in that relationship was so intense that he could have handcuffed her with a piece of bubblegum.

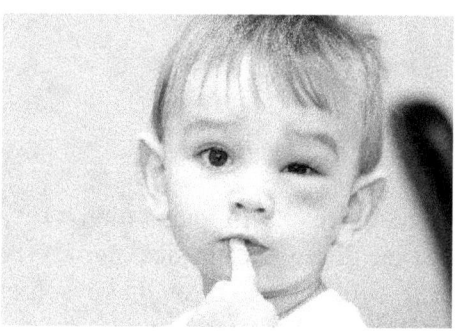

Psychological pain is every bit as debilitating (sometimes worse)   but nowhere near as understood.

Emotional Pain

How do you diagnose or measure emotional pain; we talk about heartbreak and we know that it has no connection to the organ that pumps in your chest; we know it is not a physical phenomenon but we also know that gut wrenching feeling of having your heart broken.

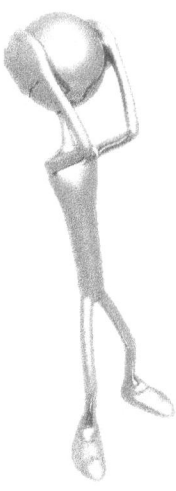

When someone you love leaves or hurts you; rejects or just fails to love you back, it hurts in a very tangible, physical way. Generally emotional pain is 'fixed' only by things like 'time', being comforted by a significant other or sometimes you just get distracted by life and what comes next!

There are no pills for emotional pain although often people will use drugs and/or alcohol… at best a short term fix or anesthetic but more often these just wear off and make you feel worse. Of course chocolate and/or ice cream have been known to work wonders.

We are human, we will feel emotional pain BUT you can most definitely speed up the recovery process with the same techniques I have given you for physical pain and for self-esteem, anxiety and abandonment issues.

In terms of prevention: the stronger your sense of self, the better the relationship you have with yourself and the more you learn to accept and express your emotions, the less likely you are to drag out the pain of emotional wounds.

Use it or lose it!

I'm now going to upset some doctors and some physiotherapists everywhere:

PEOPLE REST TOO MUCH when they are sick and injured!

Apart from the fact that you mostly recover much faster when you are busy and working; injuries to joints and muscles need to get some controlled gentle movement/exercise as soon as possible after injury. Often when people pull a muscle or hurt a rotator cuff in the gym, they go straight into non movement!

By all means check with your physio/doctor first for your particular injury, but in many cases slow gentle appropriate movement will hasten rehabilitation.

Too much bed rest allows your system to get lazy, your circulation could be affected and your muscles and joints tend to tighten up and lose their flexibility.

So very many people use age as an excuse for being less active and involved: It's not the years it's the mindset and the choices you make; especially buying into the things that you think you can't or shouldn't do because of your age.

I want to give you a very brief lesson on an important technique (more in Magical Mind); you have heard of visualization and may still put it in the 'mung bean and hippy beads' category: it is actually quite scientifically based though.

Essentially your mind works with picture and images rather than words/thoughts. Some people will say they cannot visualize, especially colors, but you can certainly remember seeing a 'red' fire truck or a 'green' plant right? And it is extremely rare for a person not to be able to **remember in color!** So you can put colored pics in your head; if not then black and white will do.

People visualize things they do not want to happen on a daily basis; the worn out old example that people seem to relate well to is someone playing golf… tell them NOT to aim for the bushes, say it a couple of times and chances are their focus will go to the bushes and so will their golf ball.

Bike riders know that if they keep looking at a ditch they will end up in it. If every time you walk past the stairs you think "I am going to fall down those one day" you will keep putting that picture in your head and ultimately program yourself to do so.

When you keep putting pics in your head, even if your saying, 'I don't want to trip' or 'fall off my bike', your mind keeps imagining that scenario but without the 'don't'. You can't really picture something NOT happening now can you?

Fortunately you need to visualize something with reasonable intensity (depending on what it is) for it to manifest; given the negativity you see and hear from people it's a good thing that it isn't instant.

But like everything else I tell you, this is knowledge you can turn around to your benefit. First of course; stop putting images of what you don't want in your head!

That is not as easy as it sounds because if I tell you NOT to think of blue hippopotamuses, especially not a big blue hippopotamus holding a daisy… etc. , NOW try to stop thinking about him…..And whatever you do…DO NOT get that picture in your head!

If I now say OK you can think about your big blue hippo OR you can think about something else, you have a choice, and you can now put something else in your head. Minds tend not to like being empty and it's really hard to stop thinking about something, unless you replace it with something else.

OK so now you know what visualization is and that you can do it; how does it fit into a book about pain?

What about pain that is being inflicted on you, like getting a tattoo or being at the dentist, getting stitches out, whatever. While you are focused on what is happening you are going to feel it with way more intensity than if you take your mind, and all your senses, elsewhere. I always tell the dentist or the tattoo guy, don't talk to me because I'm going to leave for a while.

The more you get into your 'other place' 'fantasy' whatever, the less you will be aware of the pain.

Same as when you are using visualization to create something in your life, the more detail you use the more real it becomes.

One of my tattoos took a couple of hours and I went off into fairyland, engaged all of my senses in that I could see, hear, smell, touch everything in my fantasy world (like meditation and daydreaming). Time goes by really quickly and when it's time to come back it is as though you have been asleep/dreaming/somewhere else.

I once used this technique to have dental surgery without anesthetic (just to prove I could) it worked, except the nurse kept interrupting me to ask if I was sure I did not want a needle, of course every time she did this I felt what was going on. I proved my point so these days I go for the needle – it's less work.

But I still do it for other stuff, use it in conjunction with things like numbing gel etc. and you will have pretty good pain control. I don't know how women put up with waxing, or why, when we have easy pain free creams, but they do. Maybe they use this technique?

Emotional pain and painful memories are still pain even though you're not being cut up or smacked around.

These things are largely covered in my other books but essentially the same things apply in terms of distraction, getting busy and focusing on something else.

But if it is something that still eats away at you then you need to look at the cause; break it down, why does it still hurt?

Is it because you need answers? Is it because you want revenge, satisfaction, closure, resolution?

You will never get answers unless you know exactly what your questions are.

List them; what are the possible answers (Everything you can possibly think of no matter how bizarre). What answer would satisfy you? Make you happy? Let you put an end to this pain?

Is it even possible for the other party to give you an answer that would work for you? Would it change the outcome? Would it change the past? Or the future?

How would each possible scenario change who you are, what you do, how you are going to live tomorrow?

Most of these answers you can work out for yourself, some you will never get: are you going to throw away the rest of your life on worrying about something about which you really do not have all the information.

Maybe you can get the information you need, if so DO IT!

Don't waste another day unless you're prepared to take whatever action you may need in order to get your answers BUT if you can't then maybe it's time to take your life back and move on.

Sometime people waste their entire lives stewing over past events that were out of their control. You only need to know how these past issues impact on you now, how is your attitude and behavior towards your 'self', your relationships, your life, affected by emotional pain from the past.

If you are experiencing emotional pain in your current situation, what can you do to change it?

Examine what it is that is holding you back and get help to either change your situation and/or change how you respond to it.

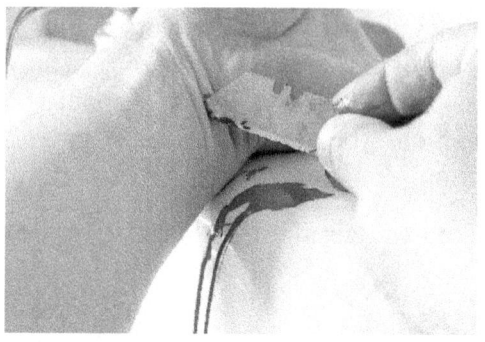

Self-harming isn't just cutting   and it is not necessarily a suicide attempt (but of course can be) very few really understand self-abuse, ironically cutting gets most of the stigma when people have many ways of self-harming that hardly get noticed.

Drug and alcohol abuse may be more socially acceptable than cutting, less dramatic maybe? But not that different! And let us not forget Food Abuse!

Over the years I have worked with 100s of serious self-harmers; some were of course teenage girls cutting arms and legs but many were men, clients of all ages, a lot of women in their 40s. I would not say men do it less only that we are less likely to find out about it. The men I have seen usually cut their abdomen or inner thighs; having said that, men tend to be more likely toward completed suicide because historically they are less inclined to see a psychologist or tell someone they need help. Having said that; over the last decade or so we have seen the numbers of men coming to therapy improve (increase) tremendously!

Men also are more likely to be sneaky about self-harming; like getting into a bar fight where the odds (or size of the other guy) guarantee a decent beating.

Anyone can have problems but it takes guts to get help and address them!

It is almost guaranteed that people who self-harm have some sort of abuse in their past. It is not unlike eating disorders in that the harming is seen as a way of having pain they can control; often seeing the blood run is a way of releasing emotional pain (not the best way of course but just to help you understand why they do it).

For many it also serves the purpose of punishment for deep seated irrational guilt (generally for things that were never their fault in the first place). Too often people who self-harm are put in the 'too hard' basket and/or labelled as "personality disorders" and even health professionals give up on them.

Great, because this feeds right into an already damaged 'self' that thinks it is not worth anything anyway.

If you self-harm or know anyone who does; get them to a good therapist! There has been a trend of late where some young girls start cutting because someone on Facebook suggested that it might help; one of the many many examples of what makes Facebook potentially dangerous.

Prevention is always better than cure

You have a fire extinguisher in the kitchen even though you don't plan on setting a fire right? You have car insurance hopefully! How much do you do to insure your ongoing fitness, mobility and health requirements? Like so many thing, we often want the benefit but don't want to go to any effort to make them happen.

In 'The Little Book to be Physically Phabulous' I go into everything you need to do to look and feel healthy and attractive: But in terms of pain there are many things you can do to protect yourself:

Exercise: No that doesn't just mean pay a gym membership you have no intention of using or buy a piece of exercise equipment from late night TV.

Seriously does anyone believe that there is a gadget that is going to give them rock'in abs in 2 minutes?

IF you are going to lose 100 pounds overnight you're going to get extremely sick! (Even if it were possible). BUT exercise means moving your body! There are ways of moving your body that you enjoy!

Even if you only play pool, you can do muscle exercises at the same time; someone the other day said they did not exercise but their sole means of transport is a bicycle…uh.. That's really good exercise! So is dancing, water sports, walking, sex, as I said-   'moving your body!

USE IT OR LOSE IT (not rocket science) people often avoid exercise because they say they have no energy OR their joints don't work OR it hurts...

They are all really good reasons......

To DO exercise!

NOT to avoid it!

I know of cases where a person has complained about perceived aches and pains and illnesses all their life only to end up getting them 'for real' when they were older!   Coincidence I guess!

Your choice, get old, immobile and in pain, or get active!

Of course you don't have to!!!

It is a choice!

Just don't say you can't, instead say you chose not to (be real!)

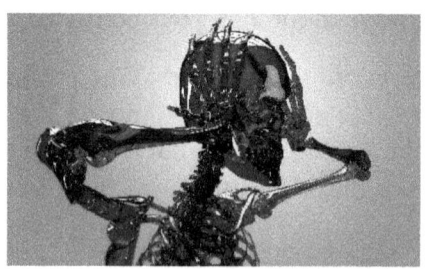

If you have weak (or unused) joints or muscles ask a physio or a gym junky or better still a personal trainer if you can afford it (they are great and better value for money than what you spend on alcohol or shoes) to help you sort out gentle consistent exercises to build up strength and stamina.

Eat!   Your car won't run without fuel! Your phone will stop if you don't charge it! You know how you feel if you don't sleep! So why would you think you can be energetic and healthy if you don't feed your body. You water and feed the plants in your garden and that works right! Your body is a machine, and a damn good one at that (few design flaws admittedly) but if you want high performance keep up the maintenance.

People get sick and die when they don't have to!

It is crazy how many people don't get things checked out by the doctor "in case it turns out to be bad..." that's just dumb!

The sooner you know about something the better the odds of fixing it; getting your boobs checked for cancer isn't going to put the cancer there! These days cancer is not necessarily a death sentence; stupidity can be though!

True story (long one cut short): When I had breast cancer another family member started to get some sympathy pains, but she had been checked out only weeks before so there was nothing to worry about... WRONG, thankfully, she wasn't stupid so she got it checked out again anyway.

She had grown an in-operable lump in that short space of time so it turns out me getting cancer was a really good thing because I am totally fine and she got chemo in time to shrink the lump to something they could cut out, then more chemo to save her life. And we are all living happily thereafter thank you very much.

On that note, when bad stuff happens it is easy get all down and depressed, why me etc., (I do it too!) It's pretty normal and human but the above is a good example of how something that started off really bad had a good outcome. Way better to have 2 sick people recover than just have 1 die right!

It happens to all of us in less dramatic ways; we are inconvenienced or worse and we get pissed off because life sometimes just isn't fair or right. Over a decade ago I was all geared up for a holiday in Bali, beach by day, clubs by night, I was really looking forward to it. At the last minute I had to cancel because of money or some other reason, whatever. Anyway I was not happy, there certainly was no up-side to spending my vacation home alone in front of the TV.

Well that is unless you call not getting blown up at a nightclub an upside: yup, I was 'supposed' to be there that night in Bali, and the next day was to be the last day of my holiday and I would probably not have been around to catch my flight home.

We know bad stuff happens to good people BUT remember *sometimes* bad stuff happens for really good reasons!

Maybe you will find out what horror you avoided (like it being all over the news of the world) or maybe you will never know!

Next time you're pissed off because of something you wanted and did not get….. Remind yourself that maybe it was for the best and you will never even know why… maybe not, but at least you can feel better about your loss if you accept that as a possibility!   I love the expression....' probably dodged a bullet'

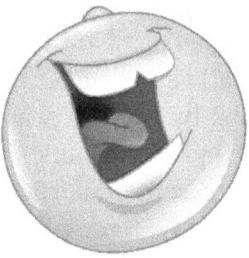

At the end of the day laughing is often the only thing that will stop you from crying!

Back to pain: There is so much you can do on a daily basis;

• Most important of all keep the pictures in your mind healthy; then go out and live as though you can!

• Where possible avoid pain meds so that when you really need them they will be of some help!

• Enjoy life, chocolate, alcohol whatever but don't be stupid!

- Channel healthy anger into energy!

- Use common sense and keep some balance.

- Moderation in all things including moderation!

- Get stuff checked by the doctor,

- Get second opinions too.

- Little things that take no time or effort

  like sunscreen and hats.

- Carry out proper maintenance on your body.

- Plan to live for decades but go out and live
  TODAY!

On vitamin supplements: people tend to go to extremes and waste a lot of money BUT it is really hard to get everything you need from food. Muscles and joints need extra help. Immune systems need taking care of.

Anything that includes words like miracle, guaranteed, overnight etc. and ends with a huge price tag tends to put me off: If something sounds too good to be true, don't be cynical but definitely take some time to check it out properly.

Does anyone seriously believe that a diet consisting of only lemon juice is a good idea! Or that eating two or three items everyday will be ok for any length of time! Common sense; seriously!

The people that buy these things aren't necessarily stupid they just really want to believe in a miracle, which is fine, but don't be a victim of marketing hype.

Wanting something to be ok won't make it so!

In Australia we do not have a lot of magnesium in our soil so there is little if any in our veggies and we definitely do need it in our diet.

Vitamin B is proven to be relevant in many health issues, especially stress as well as overuse of alcohol and other substances; vitamin C is a no brainer.

I personally swear by Krill oil tabs; I like evidence so by taking a supplement for a while then stopping to see if there is a difference I feel reasonably sure that I get benefits from what I take. The difference in my nails with Krill is evident so I am quite sure it is doing other good stuff too.

Another point on vitamins because I am not a pharmacist I like to have one or two places where I can rely on getting sound information as to what the most effective, economical and absorbable brands to purchase are.

No point in taking them if you don't do it properly and no value in spending $50 when ten will do the same job!

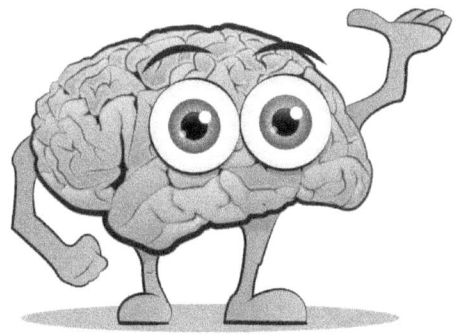

My regime (that doesn't mean it has to be the same for you) is Calcium and Magnesium tabs in the evening (I'm told it has some benefits in terms of sleep) with vitamin D depending on how much I am out in the sun; then in the morning a good multivitamin, Krill, glucosamine and I also like to use a probiotic supplement and some Bs..

I eat well most of the time but I have days when chocolate and ice cream are on the menu but never ever served up with guilt or "I really shouldn't" (see The Little Book to be Physically Phabulous). There are a lot of conflicting 'opinions' as to whether vitamins are worth spending your hard earned cash on.

At the end of the day make up your own mind using a little trial and error and a lot of common sense!

Moderation,

Balance

&

Live Life!

Love Hurts

How about 'love-pain' (don't laugh, its real, if you never felt love-pain you have not been living)

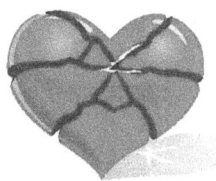

The serious relationship stuff is covered in 'Reviving Relationships', but whether you're 16 or 45 love-pain can be awful!

At 16 it's made worse by people around you minimizing your feelings as though they are not as valid because of your age.

It's real!

It hurts and it does pass!

Not meaning to sound cynical but the best cure really is a new love interest and at the end of the day if someone does not want to be with you they clearly were not the right person for you; you can do better and you will. BUT that's doesn't help at the time!

A good cry never killed anyone!

So have a cry, grieve the loss of what might have been and then get back in the ring! Truth is you probably dodged a bullet but at the very least you are now free to find someone who will love you back.

Pain is an element of life;
It can be your friend:
Without it you would not
know you need help or that
you need to make changes!
Respect your pain and
use it appropriately!
After it has served
its purpose,
Get rid of it!

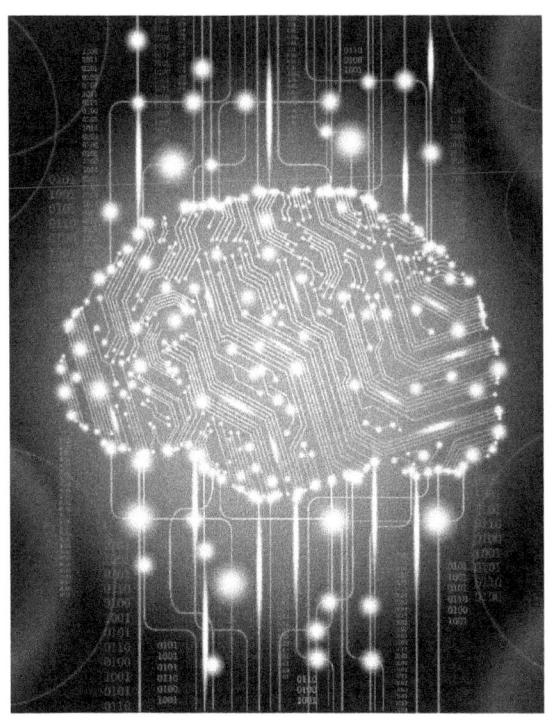

So, you enjoyed this little book?

You can discover more books
& CDs in "The Little Book" series.
www.littlebookseries.us

The Little Book & CD Series

- *Your Child the Little Scientist*
- The Little Book to Push Through Pain
- The Little Book to Annihilate Anxiety
- The Little Book to Revive Relationships
- The Little Book to Defeat Depression
- The Little Book to Salvage Self Esteem
- The Little Book to be Physically Phabulous
- Amazing Abilities of Your Magical Mind

littlebooks2013@gmail.com

www.littlebookseries.us

"The Little Book & CD" series.

 Your Child the Little Scientist

 The Little Book to Revive Relationships

 The Little Book to Annihilate Anxiety

 The Little Book to Push Through Pain

 The Little Book to Defeat Depression

 The Little Book to Salvage Self Esteem

 The Little Book to be Physically Phabulous

 Amazing Abilities of your Magical Mind

CD therapy

 Anxiety

 Alcohol

 Depression

Drugs

 Self Esteem

Smoking

 Pain

Relationships

 Abandonment

 Sleep

 Anger

 Health

www.ingramcontent.com/pod-product-compliance
Lightning Source LLC
Chambersburg PA
CBHW070822290526
45795CB00002B/815